YOUR KNOWLEDGE HAS VALUE

- We will publish your bachelor's and master's thesis, essays and papers

- Your own eBook and book - sold worldwide in all relevant shops

- Earn money with each sale

Upload your text at www.GRIN.com
and publish for free

David Salomoni

1776 - Echoes of the American Revolution in the Dukedom of Parma, Piacenza and Guastalla

GRIN Verlag

Bibliografische Information der Deutschen Nationalbibliothek:

Die Deutsche Bibliothek verzeichnet diese Publikation in der Deutschen Nationalbibliografie; detaillierte bibliografische Daten sind im Internet über http://dnb.d-nb.de/ abrufbar.

Dieses Werk sowie alle darin enthaltenen einzelnen Beiträge und Abbildungen sind urheberrechtlich geschützt. Jede Verwertung, die nicht ausdrücklich vom Urheberrechtsschutz zugelassen ist, bedarf der vorherigen Zustimmung des Verlages. Das gilt insbesondere für Vervielfältigungen, Bearbeitungen, Übersetzungen, Mikroverfilmungen, Auswertungen durch Datenbanken und für die Einspeicherung und Verarbeitung in elektronische Systeme. Alle Rechte, auch die des auszugsweisen Nachdrucks, der fotomechanischen Wiedergabe (einschließlich Mikrokopie) sowie der Auswertung durch Datenbanken oder ähnliche Einrichtungen, vorbehalten.

Imprint:

Copyright © 2012 GRIN Verlag GmbH
Druck und Bindung: Books on Demand GmbH, Norderstedt Germany
ISBN: 978-3-656-35313-3

This book at GRIN:

http://www.grin.com/en/e-book/206509/1776-echoes-of-the-american-revolution-in-the-dukedom-of-parma-piacenza

GRIN - Your knowledge has value

Der GRIN Verlag publiziert seit 1998 wissenschaftliche Arbeiten von Studenten, Hochschullehrern und anderen Akademikern als eBook und gedrucktes Buch. Die Verlagswebsite www.grin.com ist die ideale Plattform zur Veröffentlichung von Hausarbeiten, Abschlussarbeiten, wissenschaftlichen Aufsätzen, Dissertationen und Fachbüchern.

Visit us on the internet:

http://www.grin.com/

http://www.facebook.com/grincom

http://www.twitter.com/grin_com

1776
ECHOES OF THE AMERICAN REVOLUTION IN THE DUKEDOM OF PARMA, PIACENZA AND GUASTALLA

David Salomoni

The sun never shined on a cause of greater worth. 'Tis not the affair of a city, a country, a province, or a kingdom, but of a continent. 'Tis not the concern of a day, a year, or an age; posterity are virtually involved in the contest, and will be more or less affected even to the end of time, by the proceedings now.[1]

-Thomas Paine

It is with these words that, at the beginning of the year 1776, the English pamphleteer Thomas Paine defined the scope of the action undertaken by the American patriots against their homeland: England. A universal cause, the beginning of a catharsis that would involve future generations, relieving their shoulders from the burden represented by the inequalities between individuals that still the social structures of old Europe. The age of the American Revolution represented for his contemporaries, on both sides of the Atlantic Ocean, a moment of excitement and hope. There was a widespread feeling that after such event, something in the world would change. People felt like they were assisting a dramatic clash between continents, and, for the majority of the generation that in that age read the works of Voltaire and Raynal, the victorious war for independence fought by the colonies looked like the great punishment for Europe, corrupted by a seemingly dark medieval heritage. It was feared the possibility that one day America would have in turn dominated Europe. After the Declaration of Independence, the attention previously given to the events overseas added to the philosophical debate, the problems of the insertion of the nascent American state in the network of diplomatic and military relations.

The war, stretching over seven years, and looking more and more like an international conflict involving France, Spain, and Holland, risked becoming a world war. As the international community became increasingly involved in the conflict, it is possible to observe a growing awareness of the events taking place even in Italy, usually thought of as being well

---

[1] Cited in Paine, T. (2001). *Rights of Men, Common Sense and Other Political Writings*. Oxford: Oxford University Press. p. 56.

removed from the conflict. However, Italian monarchs, aristocrats, intellectuals and explorers did not remain indifferent to the struggle for independence undertaken by the American colonies. Indeed, there are many recorded relationships between significant Italian and American personalities, such as the strong amity reportedly established between the Tuscan Filippo Mazzei and Thomas Jefferson.

This work seeks to better understand how a small and, under a political perspective, seemingly insignificant northern Italian state, the Dukedom of Parma, Piacenza and Guastalla, became connected to the political and military storm brewing in a far-distant corner of the world called America. The time examined in this essay is the year 1776. During the eighteenth century the Dukedom of Parma depended both economically and politically on the two main Bourbon powers: France and Spain. France and Spain were also the two main allies of the American revolutionaries. Parma was diplomatically represented by Spain, while its only independent diplomatic representation of the small state resided in France. Nonetheless, it would not, at first consideration, seem obvious to find such a wide and detailed amount of information concerning the American Revolution, or about the parliamentary debates taking place in London, in the dukedom's only official means of communication, the *Gazzetta di Parma*. Indeed, in this period, Parma was arguably the most politically conservative state on the Italian peninsula, one unlikely to be so interested in the talk of rights and freedom being spread by the American Revolution.

The duke Don Ferdinando di Borbone, freed in 1771 from the Francophile ascendancy of his reform-minded prime minister Guillaume-Léon du Tillot, initiated a return *en arrière*.[2] Du Tillot's fall was linked with that of the French minister Choiseul who, at the time, was a main supporter of the Parmesan minister's policies.[3] Following his removal, du Tillot was replaced with the more controllable Count Giuseppe Sacco and between 1771 and 1775 Ferdinando di Borbone recalled the Jesuit order into the state and restored the Holy Inquisition.[4] Even the duke's wife, Marie Amelie of Habsburg, was intolerant to French and Spanish tutelage over the

---

[2] Tocci, G. (1979). Il ducato di Parma e Piacenza. *In:* Galasso, G. Ed. *Storia d'Italia*. Turin: UTET. Ch. XVII/1. p. 263.
[3] Ibid. pp. 307-308.
[4] Ibid. pp. 308-309.

small state and was eager to bring her husband's dukedom under imperial Austrian protection. Indeed, these years would mark a turning point that saw a crucial shift in Austria's foreign policy vis-à-vis the Italian territories. Until the first half of eighteenth century, the marriage policy followed by the Habsburgs had been oriented towards Germany and the most important royal houses of the empire. Subsequently, the policy of the House of Habsburg changed, becoming increasingly more externally oriented in accordance to evolving dynastic interests. This shift had been a long time coming and had been anticipated by certain policymakers, among them the Austrian chancellor of state, Baron Kaunitz, inventor of the *Renversement des Alliances*, which seemed to guarantee a new alliance between the Viennese court and France.[5]

With regard to the purpose of the work it is not incautious to believe that, within the political game played by the main European powers, the duke of Parma could glimpse the possibility of cutting out a wider margin of administrative power among his states for himself. It is useful to point out the political context in which the Dukedom of Parma was absorbed, in order to show how little evident was for the duke Ferdinando to follow slavishly the directions and the orientations concerning foreign policy followed by his more powerful kinsmen, the kings of France and Spain, The two branches of the Bourbons were linked by a solidarity that has seen storms at the time of the Regency, but that cemented in family pact between the Spain of Philip V and Charles III, and the France of Louis XV and Louis XVI.[6]

Within the scope of foreign and Italian historiography no research has been made on the reception of the American Revolution inside the north-central Italian states: the Dukedom of Parma, Piancenza and Guastalla and the Dukedom of Modena. This current work is meant to be the introduction to a larger study on how one of these small political entities became involved with the events that, during the last quarter of the eighteenth century, were to have a profound effect on the course of history. Despite the absence of works concerning Parma, there has been some significant research done on the reception of the American Revolution in other Italian states, fundamental for any critical work of comparison. Among these, the most complete is the fourth volume of the monumental work of Franco Venturi concerning the eighteenth century:

---

[5] Mazohl-Wallnig, B. (2005). Tra politica imperiale e politica dinastica. *In*: Mora, A. Ed. *Un Borbone tra Parma e l'Europa. Don Ferdinando e il suo tempo*. Reggio Emilia:Edizioni Diabasis, ch.3, p. 30.
[6] Ibid. Vovelle, M. (2005). Parme, de l'Europe des Lumières à l'Europe en Révolution. ch.1, p. 16.

Settecento Riformatore[7], in which relations with American patriots and local Italian states and personalities are finely analyzed. Another major volume of miscellaneous works, edited by Giorgio Spini and Tiziano Bonazzi is *Italia e America dal Settecento all'Età dell'Imperialismo*[8], containing notable essays such as "Northern America in the Archives of the Sacred Congregation 'de Propaganda Fide'," written by Luca Codignola concerning the relations between the Papal State and Catholic communities in North America; "Public Opinion in Piedmont before the American Revolution and the Making of the United States," written by Piera Ciavirella, and "Tuscan Scholars and New America in Late Eighteenth Century Academic Competition" written by Piero del Negro.

The primary sources used for this research are mostly unpublished. They are the dispatches from the ambassador of Parma at Versailles to the Parmesan secretary of state, contained in Parma's State Archive (PSA), and editions of the *Gazetta di Parma* from 1776, contained in the municipal archive.

THE REVOLUTION IN THE
GAZZETTA DI PARMA
(JANUARY-AUGUST 1776)

To all appearances all united colonies are on the eve of a glorious revolution.[9]

-*Gazzetta di Parma*, 15 May 1776

The information contained within the articles of the *Gazzetta di Parma* that concern the political and military drama of the revolution can be grouped into three main categories. The first relates to the parliamentary debate in England among radical exponents in solidarity with the American revolutionaries, supporters of a policy of openness towards the grievances of the colonies; the Old Whigs, pushed by political calculation to criticize the policy of George III in America; and the parliamentarians who supported the king and sustained a strong colonial policy

---

[7] Venturi, F. (1984). *Settecento Riformatore*. Turin: Einaudi. (The French historian Michelle Vovelle defined Venturi's *Settecento Riformatore*: « […] une référence majeure et que nombre de dix-huitièmistes on au moins effleuré comme René Poumeau et parfois decouvert […]»).

[8] Spini, G., Bonazzi, T., Eds. (1976). *Italia e America dal Settecento all'Età dell'Imperialismo*. Venice: Marsilio Editori.

[9] Unknown. (1776). Philadelphia, 15 May 1776, *Gazzetta di Parma*, 31, p. 245. (With regard to the Gazette of Parma, the authors of the articles are never mentioned. The title of the articles is always represented by the article's place and date of writing).

against the protests of the revolutionaries. The second category of news published in the small Bourbon capital city, directly relates to goings-on of war: naval battles, warfare, and the displacement of troops. The focus is especially on the Canadian campaign, begun in 1775 and resolved by the defeat of American forces during the siege of Quebec in the spring of 1776. The third category comprises news received directly from America that arrived without having gone through the mediatory filter of London, Leiden or Amsterdam – cities from which came most of Parma's foreign news. This communication channel without mediation illuminates the perspective of the American insurgents on current events. These articles describe the mood of the civilian population in America, the material conditions in which they poured and the reasons why they were driven to such a resolution, showing the first steps of a new state ready, as stated in the Declaration of Independence, "to assume among the Powers of the Earth, the separate and equal Station to which the Laws of Nature and of Nature's God entitle them."[10]

In ten years, between 1773 and 1783, a series of upheavals transformed the political landscape of British America. The Boston Tea Party of December 1773 marked a new and delicate period in the already deteriorated relationship between Britain and its continental colonies, which eventually resulted two years later in open rebellion and war.[11] The political situation in Britain, as shown by the *Gazzetta di Parma* for the year 1776, illustrates the attempt by George III to restore royal power as granted according to the principles of 1689, consolidating in his own hands the right of state patronage and embodying the ideal of the "patriotic king." A loose sheet circulating along the roads of London during 1776, and reported in the gazette, appeals to the king: "Arise, O king order a fasting for Great Britain and America: end the bloodshed of your children."[12] The position held by George III arose from the Glorious Revolution of 1689, which confirmed the political prominence of parliament and depicted the monarch as a father to his subjects. This political model was particularly close to the role that Duke don Ferdinando wished to embody in his own state, small though it was.

---

[10] Maier, P., ed. (1998). *The Declaration of Independence and The Constitution of the United States*. New York: Bantam Books, p. 53.
[11] Elliot, J. (2006). *Empires of the Atlantic World. Britain and Spanish America 1492-1830*. Turin: Einaudi, p. 475.
[12] Unkonwn. (1776). London, 5 march 1776, *Gazzetta di Parma*, 10, pp. 76-77.

However, for the American subjects of the British Crown, the alliance between the King and the Parliament became unbearable when, after the Seven Years' War, the British Empire sought to reorganize its administrative and financial architecture, affecting some of the privileges held by the colonies in respect of taxes.

The Declaration of Independence evoked principles that were familiar to political philosophers of the time, but that became revolutionary only in the moment that they were expressed in public documents. The principles expressed in the Declaration of Independence can move between the theoretical plan of philosophy and the pragmatic plan of politics due to rhetoric and epistemology that hold and connects directly these two plans.[13] What we find in the Declaration of Independence is a symbolic regicide, an act that in the political culture of the eighteenth century had destructive psychological and symbolic meanings.[14] Despite the fact that this reasoning seems to grow in importance when related to the political mentality expressed by one of the most conservative Italian states of the late eighteenth century, we are faced with some startling evidence of openness to the rebel cause, such as a letter sent from the local Congress of North Carolina to London that was reproduced in Parma on 19 March 1776:

> If moderation, which is seen in all acts issued by the General Congress in Philadelphia, seems to refute the reproaches of an unbridled enthusiasm, that the opponents of the colonies assume in all resolutions and drawings of Americans, also the acts of local congresses or special assemblies can be used to justify them from the aims of independence, with which they are generally charged. It is remarkable in this sort, a letter that the provincial congress of North Carolina wrote to the inhabitants of the British Empire, and is as follows: friends and fellow citizens, the outcome of the dispute, there is now between the American colonies and the British ministers will determine one of the most important eras of English history.[15]

Despite the fact that the publication of this letter precedes the Declaration of Independence, it shows how events were followed carefully inside the Dukedom of Parma.

---

[13] Bonazzi, T., ed. (2003). *La Dichiarazione di indipendenzadegli Stati Uniti d'America*. Venezia: Marsilio Ed., p. 23.
[14] Ibid. p. 24.
[15] Unknown. (1776). London, 19 march 1776, *Gazzetta di Parma*, 12, pp. 91-94.

Within the letter from the congress of North Carolina the accusation of aspiring to independence is refused repeatedly. This safeguarding of the king – still considered by many in 1775 to be the father of his subjects, despite the constitutionally limited nature of his power – meant defending the ancient association between political community and family, a concept also familiar to the Duke of Parma and his own subjects, a great majority of which there to be only chaos absent the role of the royal patriarch. Moreover, a republican alternative, following the Cromwellian experiment, was considered to be a frightening *damnatio memoriae* in the minds of the English.[16] The text proceeds reporting that:

> Foreign nations expect these results with restless curiosity and watch with amazement the blind and obstinate policy with which this administration insists on his plan to subjugate these colonies and to reduce them by the state of loyal and useful subjects to an absolute dependence and vilest slavery; as if the descendants of those ancestors who have shed rivers of blood and spent treasures to establish the freedom of the British Constitution on a solid and permanent base, saw with envious eyes the happy state of this nation in the West and they tried to exterminate the models of those virtues which shone with a radiance that was feared to be equal or outshine them.[17]

Despite its rhetorical tone, a crucial issue inherent in British constitutionalism is introduced in this part of the text. It in fact gives a nod, brief but illuminating, to the fact that the path followed during those weeks by the American colonies, which would lead shortly afterwards to the declaration made on of 4 July, was completely internal to the English political and legal tradition. It was clear, also in Parma, that the sidpute between the Colonies and the Mother Country was related to a constitutional issue. Where was, now, the British constitution, perfectly balanced, with all its checks and balances, when the legislative power which had overthrown the tyrants had itself become tyrannical? Why was the king, natural protector of his people, not assisting them in their time of need? These disturbing questions were on the minds of many British American subjects in the decade between 1765 and 1775[18] and such unsettling truths

---

[16] Bonazzi, T., ed. (2003). *La Dichiarazione di indipendenzadegli Stati Uniti d'America*. Venezia: Marsilio Ed., p. 25.
[17] Unknown. (1776). London, 19 march 1776, *Gazzetta di Parma*, 12, pp. 91-94.
[18] Elliot, J. (2006). *Empires of the Atlantic World. Britain and Spain America 1492-1830*. Turin: Einaudi, p. 475.

forced them to make decisions that, until only a few years previously they would have never dreamed of making. This pervasive mood is clearly shown within the articles reported in the *Gazzetta:*

> Enjoy the fruits of our honest industry, be able to call our own good what we gain with the work of our hands and the sweat of our brows, have the right to regulate our affairs, that is the great grace we ask! The names of traitors and rebels and many other insulting epithets, suggested by hatred, and uttered with the tongue biting are the answer that we receive for the most humble and pressing demands and petitions. We are warned that we do not aspire but to independence, that we try to break all the bonds that unite us to the mother country. Oh cruel accusation! All our protests and all our actions do not prove uniformly to the contrary?[19]

Faced with these accusations, it is not surprising that British Americans felt under siege by a Europe that claimed to be enlightened. The fresh vitality of the New World, which European critics considered to a weakness, could, on the contrary, be considered a great strength. If the Old World looked to the past, the New World was looking at the future. These contrasting images burned themselves into the collective consciousness of the colonists. Although they harbored a growing disillusionment with the homeland, they had proved able to stock a strong ideological arsenal with which to withstand the onslaught that awaited them. For a long time the population of the British colonies had access – through books, pamphlets and other publications imported from England – to a wide range of political views. These ranged from the sweeping views of the Tory statesman Bolingbroke that had passed through the orthodox doctrines of the Whig government and rested comfortably on the constitutional foundations established by the Glorious Revolution, to the doctrines of the radical libertarian seventeenth and eighteenth-century Commonwealthmen John Trenchard and Thomas Gordon. These different political visions of society, generated by the fractures and upheavals of the English Civil War and the Glorious Revolution, had crossed the Atlantic to the colonial community in America. With each of these shocks came a new explosion of political debate. The echoes of such a heated political landscape arrived in Parma as well. For example, the excited words of the radical John Wilkes are reported:

---

[19] Unknown. (1776). London, 19 march 1776, *Gazzetta di Parma*, 12, pp. 91-94.

> You have granted the preparation of fleets and armies that do the most good on paper, but this is still not enough to subjugate America. The Congress of Americans does not pay a regular salary, as we do, to a bureaucracy that costs 140 million pounds. The Congress has not a host of hungry officials and creatures to satiate. Every shilling that will arise from that country must be spent for the benefit of that country. America is like a young boy, who came to strength, with substantial assets and not aggravated by debt. We, on the contrary, we are like a sick voluptuous, whose forces are exhausted by debauchery, who lives on credit and who owes more than he can pay.[20]

It was a radical belief that if parliament had actually represented the British people, including settlers, America would not have separated. The gazette also witnesses the feelings of part of the British population. Popular discontent was caused by the extra-parliamentary debates held by Whigs members, able to exploit the frustration of small merchants caused by the withdrawal of American orders for goods in reaction to the duties imposed on imports. To this is added, with the coercive laws of 1775, the prohibition of British subjects to trade with the rebellious colonies, putting many small merchants into a state of prostration. News of March 1776 from London indicates that the ambassadors of Lord North in America had failed to reach an agreement with the revolutionary leaders and the Americans were enlisting men and preparing to resist. It is clear from the content of the subsequent news from London, as reported in the *Gazzetta di Parma*, that all of British's hopes to save the situation was now lost:[21]

> Special notices from America say that little by little the form of government adopted by the United Colonies, takes consistency, which means that they will not desist easily from the concerted plan. So fades inexorably any hope of reconciliation.[22]

> The dispatches received at court from America reported that both sides were given final instructions to the deepest assault and the most obstinate resistance.[23]

---

[20] Unknown. (1776). London, 2 January 1776, *Gazzetta di Parma*, 5, p. 39.
[21] Unknown. (1776). London, 12 March 1776, *Gazzetta di Parma*, 11, pp. 85-86.
[22] Unknown. (1776). London, Tuesday 9 July 1776, *Gazzetta di Parma*, 24, p. 221.
[23] Unknown. (1776). London, Tuesday 23 July 1776, *Gazzetta di Parma*, 30, p. 236.

The second strand of news reported in the pages of the *Gazzetta di Parma* about the political earthquake that struck the British Empire relates strictly to military events. The most important fact within the pages of the magazine is the Canadian campaign, conducted between the winter of 1775 and the spring of 1776. Following the battles of Lexington and Concord, the leaders of the revolution were firmly convinced that the fate of Canada was inextricably linked with that of the rest of the continent, despite the will of the Continental Congress not to launch attacks against the Canadian colony. This will, however, proved insufficient before the beliefs of officers like Colonel Benedict Arnold and General Richard Montgomery, who were confident that such an expedition would be easy and successful. One of the principle reasons put forward was that an assault on Canada would inhibit Britain's ability to launch an attack from across the northern border. An expeditionary force of 8,000 men was set up[24].

However, the most interesting category of news concerning the Revolution is that which directly came from the American colonies. Within these documents we find the first attempts at constitutional development, the political liturgies which were to found a new identity. In two separated editions of the *Gazzetta di Parma* published in January 1776 there news that seems to anticipate the future content of the Articles of Confederation and Eternal Union. Commonly known as the Articles of Confederation, this document was the first constitutional charter of the United States of America and assembled the colonies into a new federal sovereign state.

"From America.

Here's the plan, that the Congress of the continent has proposed to Provincial Assemblies of the 13 United Provinces, because they accept to transfer in it all their privileges and, with the approval of the Articles, ratify the maximum designed for the erection of a free state. And, although the same is to leave some of the usual formalities, the date, and the subscription, however there is so little reason to doubt its authenticity because such a step had been predicted since long and expected from all over Europe, and with astonishment of this number only by the Great-British Parliament seems never to have been believed, in spite of the protests of the opposition party. Still, the league made with this plan, must keep still only up to the extent that everything is put on the ancient foot revocation acts of

---

[24] Unkonwn. (1776). *Gazzetta di Parma*, 19-32, pp. 52-212.

Parliament, and compensated for the damage done to Boston, Charlestown, Falmouth c., Until eternity[25]."

A dispatch coming from Philadelphia left no hope for reconciliation:

GENTLEMEN,

In a time where, according to all appearances all united Colonies are on the eve of a glorious revolution [...] it is necessary to instruct you on different objects, so that you know the behavior you have to take in order to carry out your duty. We have seen the humble Pleas of these Colonies to the King of Great-Britain repeatedly rejected with indignation: we asked for peace, and we were offered the sword of war, in behalf of liberty presented us with chains, and in exchange for security, the death. The tools of a hostile oppression are allowed to take from us our goods, to burn our homes, and to dispel our blood. [...] In a word, we are convinced that the Ministry and Parliament of that Island have taken the absolute and invariable resolution to win, and subjugate the Colonies, to which the People of Great-Britain is Let no way willing to oppose . It seems that a reconciliation with them is so dangerous as it is absurd. [...] We believe, therefore, that it is absolutely impracticable, that the Colonies could ever be more likely, or dependent on Great-Britain, without endangering the existence of the state. Nevertheless, placing a boundless confidence in the counsels of Congress, we are determined to wait, and with endless patience, until such time, as his wisdom feel the need to declare independence. We would have never ventured to expose our feelings about this object, without the attention, that Congress would want to be backed by the Inhabitants of the Colonies all before adopting a resolution is important to each of them. As a result of the Inhabitants of this City we decide unanimously, [...] that it is necessary for the safety of the United Colonies to declare them independent of Great-Britain, the Inhabitants of this Colonies are generously willing to sacrifice their lives, and the rest of 'their assets to support this resolution.[26]

---

[25] Unknown. (1776). London, Tuesday 6 February 1776, *Gazzetta di Parma,* 6, pp. 46-47.

[26] Unknown. (1776). London, Tuesday 30 July 1776, *Gazzetta di Parma,* 31, pp. 244-245.

DIPLOMATIC CORRESPONDENCE
(OCTOBER-DECEMBER 1776)

L'Amerique ainsi libre et voyant sa population augmenteé par l'arrivé de ces emigrants, deviendra la plus florissante partie du monde entier.[27]

- Anonymous British Officer, October 1776

The second channel through which the Bourbon court of Parma was informed about the events in America was the correspondence that the Ambassador of Parma in Versailles, the Count d'Argental, maintained with the prime minister of the Duchy, Count Giuseppe Sacco. It was a news channel completely different from that of the *Gazzetta*, reserved for small public personalities of the court. The dispatches of the Ambassador of Parma usually arrived weekly or, more rarely, twice a week, and were a continuation of the previous correspondence held with the predecessor of Count Sacco, the former prime minister du Tillot. These dispatches contain information on the most important events that occurred in Europe during the week, echoes of which came to the court at Versailles. The news concerning America did not fail to provide interesting details: military encounters, debates on the impact of the war on trade and the economy, testimonies of military heroism and the insightful reflections of anonymous combatants, as well as the official speeches of ambassadors. It should be noted that it was particular that a small court like Parma should even be diplomatically represented in such a crucial site as Versailles. The merit of this presence can be attributed to Luise Elisabeth de Bourbon, daughter of King Louis XV of France, duchess consort of Don Ferdinando's father, Philip of Bourbon. There is yet another thing that is not as obvious as it would seem: the interest shown by Parma towards the events in America, especially when one recalls the attitude shown by the Spanish court towards the American ambassador John Jay a few years later. In Jay's correspondence with Samuel Huntington one reads:

> The people in this country are in almost total darkness about us. Scarce any American publications have reached them, nor are they informed of the most recent and important events in that country. The affairs of Stony Point, Paulus Hook, etc., etc., had never been

---

[27]Parma State Archive (PSA). Bourbon Foreign Correspondence (France). Envelope 65 (1776-1778). Dossier d'Argental, Bulletins des Nouvelles 1776-8th-January/1776-30th-December. Dispatch 1776-7th-October.

heard of here, except perhaps by the great officers of state, and they could scarcely believe that the Roman Catholic religion was even tolerated there.

There are violent prejudices among them against us. Many of them have even serious doubts of our being civilized, and mention a strange story of a ship driven into Virginia by distress, about thirty years ago, that was plundered by the inhabitants, and some of the crew killed in a manner and under circumstances which, if true, certainly indicate barbarity. The King and Ministry are warm, yet I have the reason to believe that the bulk of the nation is cold toward us. They appear to me like the English, hate the French, and to have prejudices against us.[28]

Spain, indeed, along with France, had the patronage on Parma's foreign policy, since the duke of Parma was a Spanish *Infante* and a member of the Bourbon family. Spain felt that France had been too precipitate in allying herself with America. As Charles III's chief minister, Grimaldi had said earlier in the war: "The right of all sovereigns to their respective territories ought to be regarded as sacred, and the example of a rebellion is too dangerous to allow of His Majesty's wishing to assist openly."[29] Floridablanca, who succeeded to Grimaldi's post in 1777, distrusted the United States even more than he feared England. Under pressure from France's minister Vergennes, Spain finally agreed to the secret Convention of Aranjuez of 12 April 1779. Spain was now ready to go to war alongside of France. The bait was Gibraltar, then in British hands.[30] However, there was a clear conflict of interest considering that actions taken by the Spanish court might risk starting a revolt in its own colonial possessions. In Europe, indeed, the middle and final decades of the seventeenth century were marked by profound changes in the balance of international power. In the Americas, where the consequences of these changes were suffered most acutely, the same period witnessed the consolidation of colonial societies as particular systems with unique characteristics that differed profoundly from the metropolitan societies from which they were born and posed fundamental problems of identity that would become more pressing during the eighteenth century. The monopoly of the New World granted to the Iberian monarchs by Alexander VI in 1493 thus lost the last remnants of its legitimacy.

---

[28] Jay to the President of Congress. 1 - The Correspondence and Public Papers of John Jay, vol. 1 (1763-1781). The Online Library of Liberty. Consulted on December 1st, 2012. http://oll.libertyfund.org/
[29] Commager, H.S. and Morris, R.B., eds. (1967). *The Spirit of Seventy-Six*. New York: Harper and Row Publisher, p. 991.
[30] Ibid. p. 990.

Although the Spanish crown continued to keep the bulk of its possessions in the Americas and fleets kept coming year after year to the Iberian peninsula with cargos of silver, there was a widespread impression that Spain itself was in a phase of final decline. If Spain in the sixteenth century was a model to follow it was the model to avoid. The stimulus to trade, so neglected by the Spaniards, began to be regarded as central to the interests of other countries, first of all, Britain.[31] It is of fundamental importance to underline the attitude shown by Spain toward the American Revolution in order to establish the particularity of Parma's interest. In the dispatches arriving from Paris there is both official and personal evidence of the on-going conflict. Within the most interesting documents emerging from the diplomatic correspondence there are the two texts: the first is the transcription of a letter written by an anonymous British officer at the order of General Howe and the second is a speech held by the ambassador of the newly formed American congress at Versailles, John Adams. The American Revolution coincided with the peak of the Enlightenment and was a product of that climate. Many both in Europe and in America saw in the independence of the American colonies from Britain a lesson and an encouragement for humanity. With the Revolution it became evident that the liberal ideals of the Enlightenment could be put into practice. The Revolution demonstrated that the principles of human rights, the social contract, freedom, equality, responsibility of citizens and the sovereignty of the people, freedom of religion, thought and speech, separation of the powers, and written constitutions, did not apply only in theory, but could become, in that historical moment, a real political system.

The British officer, after describing in detail the poor living conditions of British soldiers and the difficulties they encountered in a hostile country ready to resist at all costs, urges his compatriots to reflect upon the reasons that pushed them into a bloody war, the outcome of which, in his view, is predetermined:

> Au nom de la paix, du commerce et de la reputation de la Grande-Bretagne, je conjure tous les anglois de mettre de coté tout préjujés, des considerer merement les faits de cette

---

[31] Elliot, J. (2006). *Empires of the Atlantic World. Britain and Spain America 1492-1830*. Turin: Einaudi, pp. 323-326.

malheureuse éxpedition, et de chercher de mettre fin a nos misères, en ramenant la paix et en travaillant a la prosperité des deux pays.[32]

The anonymous officer makes a prediction, whose foresight is remarkable. He, after considering the characteristics of America and its inhabitants, spoken language, venerable principles and social customs, as all being very similar to Britain's, states that America enjoys a true freedom unknown in any other European country and prophesies that many in Europe will be tempted to settle there. He refers specifically to Irish and Scottish Roman Catholics. Ireland and Scotland, and Ireland in particular, were the poorest areas of the United Kingdom. In Ireland, of a total population estimated at 4,500,000 inhabitants, approximately 3,000,000 were Roman Catholics. Despite the fact that in 1765 a Catholic committee was formed that would become important in the future Irish Catholics within Britain did not enjoy political rights and could not vote nor be elected to parliament and did not have access to lucrative positions or professions. Additionally, the economic conditions of the Catholics were generally poor and defined in most cases by extreme poverty. While the Industrial Revolution began in England towards the end of the eighteenth century, Ireland, despite its proximity, was generally excluded from this phenomenon, save for the northwest where the production of linen was industrialized. Furthermore, increases in exports led Irish producers to devote more land to the cultivation of exportable products and less for the production of consumable produce.

> Une grande partie de l'Ecosse, la moitié de l'Irlande n'attendent peut-être que cet evenement, opprimés par les grands et negligés par les gouvernements, les irlandais sourtout, voleront sur les ailes de l'impatience, vers ces climats heureux, ou l'abondance et une jouissance tranquille leur promettent le sort le plus doux.[33]

Thus, the British officer adds that not only would the masses of Ireland and Scotland be attracted to the abundance of the earth and the fertility of the fields in America, but also those liberal nobles and those proud spirits who in this period seemed to make liberty their own religion. In this way, portends the officer, America, with an increasing population and a people defined by

---

[32] Parma State Archive (PSA). Bourbon Foreign Correspondence (France). Envelope 65 (1776-1778). Dossier d'Argental, Bulletins des Nouvelles 1776-8th-January/1776-30th-December. Dispatch 1776-7th-October.
[33] Ibid.

industriousness and courage, will become the most prosperous land in the world, with no country able to dominate on it.

> Quelques un d'un rang plus elevé les y suivront bien tot, pour aller chercher une liberté qu'ils idolatrent, et qu'ils ne trouvent plus dans leur patrie. L'Amerique ainsi libre et voyant sa population augmentée par l'arrivé de ces emigrants, deviendra la plus florissant partie du monde entier. Trop formidable et trop puissante par avoir rien a redouter de ses ennemis, elle connaitra trop le bonheur de jouir, pour vouloir troubler le repos de ceux qu'elle ne craint point, et dont elle peut se passer.[34]

This set of expectations can also be found in John Adams's speech, made in December 1776 at the court of Versailles. The speech is fully contained in the d'Argental dispatch dated December 9, 1776:

> Nous sommes assemblés aujourd'hui pour mettre en execution ce que les hommes les plus sages et les plus vertueux se font un bonheur de contempler en idée, ce jour doit presenter au monde le spectacle le plus auguste dont les annales ayent fait mention, le spectacle de quelques millions d' hommes libres qui de leur propre volonté se forment en societé pour la defense commune et le bonheur general.[35]

Adams explains how in America a new political system no longer derived from the ancient heritage that still burdened most of the European states was about to arise for the first time in history:

> Les monarchies electives sont éxposées aux convultions, les gouvernements hereditaires manquent souvent de sagesse, de fermeté et de vertus , nous n'aurons aucun de ces inconvenients a craindre, c'est a nous à perpetuer une legislation prudente, active et juste qui ne perira que lors que nous perdrons nous même cette vertu qui en est la base; c'est ainsi nos frères et concitoyens que la providence nous permet de jouir d'un Empire fondè par la justice et le consentement d'un peuple libre; un Empire ou l'homme reprendra tous

---

[34] Ibid.
[35] Parma State Archive (PSA). Bourbon Foreign Correspondence (France). Envelope 65 (1776-1778). Dossier d'Argental, Bulletins des Nouvelles 1776-8th-January/1776-30th-December. Dispatch 1776-9th-December.

ses droits, exercera toutes ses facultés precieuses qui sont le plus beau appanage de l'espece humaine, outre les avantages de la liberté et d'une constitution Egale.[36]

Within Adams's words a powerful political myth arises. Political power, in Adams's speech, is based on the consent of a free people: "nous sommes le seul peuple qui d'un consentement libre, formé et deliberé se soit réuni par un pact social."[37] Here, the American people become the politic body, the source of legitimacy of power and true sovereignty. The only distinctions between citizens, Adams explains, will be represented by talent and personal skills.

> Icy la naissance et les richesses ne donnent pas un droit d'autorité hereditaire, pour servir la chose publique , il ne faut d'autre titre parmi nous que du zele et du talent, voila la seule distinction que nous connoissons, c'est celle de la nature.[38]

Adams's speech ends with a heartfelt denunciation of tyranny and inequities suffered by the American people at the hands of England over the decades:

> Les legions de nos ennemies couvrent nos plaines, leur route est marqué par le sang, la mort et la desolation, voyez les corps dechirés des vos compatriotes: leur blessures, ces bouches eloquentes ne vous disent elles pas: quoi! souffriréz vous que notre posterité gemisse dans les sang de nos meurtrés, nôtre sang versé en vain, notre constance jusqu'au depart n'est donc pas servi qu'a augmenter l'esclavage de notre patrie, quels sont les hommes qui vous demandent que vous leur soyez soumis, que vous obeissiés a leur decret; ce sont les mêmes hommes qui ont oubliés qu'il etaient vos frères par le sang, et que vous aviez rendu a leur une soumission longue et aveugle; qui ont oublié les sacrifices que vous aviez fait pour leur avarice; vous et vos ancetres , en leur abandonnant tout l'avantage du commerce, ce sont les même hommes qui ont formé un plan reflechi de vous depoïllier du peux de proprieté qu'ils nous avaient permis d'aquerir, souvenéz vous que les hommes qui demandent avant de gouverner, sont ceux qui conformement a leur plan de despotism , ont annullé le contract sacré fait avec vos ancetres; qui ont conduit dans nos villes une soldatesque mercenaire, qui ont voulu vous forcer a la

---

[36] Ibid.
[37] Ibid
[38] Ibid.

soumission par l'injustice et le meutre, qui ont traité votre patience de lacheté, et votre pitié d'hypocrisie.[39]

Adams's speech, as reported by the pen of d'Argental, provided the court of Don Ferdinando with all the rhetorical drama of the conflict on the American side of the Atlantic. However, the precise reaction of the duke and his officials to these fateful events remains unknown. Few sources exist that can give any clear indication of the court's official opinion however, what existing sources do certainly show is that the ducal court was well aware of the events and debates surrounding the birth of the United States of America and that the major incidents of 1776 were carefully described in the pages of the *Gazzetta di Parma*, for which the dilplomatic dispatches from Versailles provide a useful complement.

Nonetheless, we can trace additional evidence the Parmesan court's interest in the American revolution through the presence of works on North American natural and political history of in the ducal library: the Biblioteca Palantina. For the period preceding the conflict the library holds two copies of the *Gazzettiere Americano*, published in Livorno in 1763. For subsequent years, there is also the significant presence in the of the *Atlante dell'America contenente le migliori carte geografiche, e topografiche delle principali città, laghi, fiumi, e fortezze del Nuovo Mondo* (Atlas of America Containing the Best Maps, and Topographic Maps of Major Cities, Lakes, Rivers, and Forts of the New World) printed in Livorno in 1777, ad well as the existence of the *Constitutions des treize états-unis de l'Amerique – À Philadelphie* printed in Paris in 1783, written by Louis Armand de la Rochefoucauld. There also exists a copy of the *Introduzione all'America, gli Stati dell'America Unita, il Canada, e la Nuova Scozia* (An Introduction to America, the States of United America, Canada and New Scotland) written by the German explorer Anton Friedrich Büsching, translated from German and printed in Venice in 1780 and the *Historia de la ultima guerra entre la Inglaterra, los Estados Unidos de America, la Francia, Espana y Holanda : desde el ano de 1775. en que se principio hasta el de 1783. en que se concluyo; con un plan exacto, y circunstanciado de todos los navios, y buques de guerra de las potencias beligerantes, que fueron apresados, quemados, echados a pique, o destruidos. Version del frances al castellano* printed in Spain in 1793. There also several copies of the *Storia della guerra della indipendenza degli Stati Uniti di America* (History of the Independence War

---

[39] Ibid.

of the United States of America) written by the Italian explorer Carlo Botta, during the first half of the nineteenth century.

The picture that emerges from the research done is not immediately self-evident. On one hand, some in the Duchy of Parma – a small, yet important center for the exchange of eighteenth-century Enlightenment ideas – undoubtedly were attracted to the resolute action undertaken by the American colonists in seeking independence from Great Britain. Within the balance of *ancien régime* European power, the small Italian state found itself protected by the powers of Bourbon France and Spain, the main allies, along with the Netherlands, of the Continental Congress and certainly maintained a privileged position in regards to receiving details of the revolution in North America. It should also be added that the Italian press depended almost entirely on the French-Dutch information circuit, which helps explain the pro-American nature of the news items published in the *Gazzetta di Parma*. Yet, the presence of such a large amount of information on the American events should no be taken for granted.

While an argument can be made for a favorable reception of news, Parma remained a relatively conservative client state of Spain in which, apart from some enthusiasm shown by the peripheral patriotic movement, there was an imposed silence placed on the American question. The court of Madrid, though actively participating in the war, was wary of expressing sincere sympathy for the cause of the revolutionaries whose expansionist interests collided directly with Spanish interests in America and the Duke of Parma was an *Infante* of Spain whose coffers relied on Madrid as its main source of economic resources to the duchy. Moreover, the king of Spain had never abdicated the right to pronounce the last word on the internal and external policy of the small duchy. Considering these , it might be reasonable to expect that the Duchy of Parma's print media would have also had an imposed silence place upon concerning the cause of the revolutionaries. After all, the American Revolution's ideological foundations denied the legitimacy of a monarch's absolute power, based on divine right, as was duke Ferdinand's.

Despite the strong bond of friendship between some major French personalities, such as the Marquis de La Fayette and Voltaire, with the leaders of the revolutionary movement, it should also be remembered that France contributed to the American war effort mainly as geopolitical maneuver against Britain. The principles of popular sovereignty and the absence of a link between throne and altar were not perceived positively among the courts of Europe, and in the Italian ones in particular. Even in the open-minded court of the Grand Duke of Tuscany, Pietro Leopoldo, there was never any doubt that a series of reforms should be carried out, but from above, by an enlightened and absolute monarch.[40] An interesting fact is the contrast between the massive presence in the Parmesan gazette of information concerning the American Revolution in 1776, and the total silence about the French Revolution from 1789 onwards. The research of local historian Alba Pessini has revealed that during the French Revolution the court of the Duchy of Parma had indeed been duly informed of any current event in Paris thanks to the dispatches sent by the Parmesan minister in France, the knight Jean-Marie De Virieu Beauvoir, successor of d'Argental who had died in 1788.[41] Thus, the decision not to publish anything on the events relating to the French Revolution should be considered a conscious decision and not a simple lack of information. Similarly, it would be legitimate to believe that the publication of news concerning the American Revolution was also a conscious choice, not forced by external pressure. It is possible to believe that the duke Ferdinand saw in the American Revolution a positive event, not fully perceiving the potential threat to his *ancien régime* order.

The limited nature of the period of time taken into account, only the year 1776, opens the possibility for further research concerning the knowledge of American events in the Duchy of Parma for the duration of the Anglo-American conflict and perhaps on the period of debate and constitutional development that followed until 1789. This would allow more complete and exhaustive conclusions to be drawn on what appears to be an interesting chapter to add to the history of transatlantic communication of information and ideas.

---

[40] Commager, H.S. and Morris, R.B., eds. (1967). *The Spirit of Seventy-Six*. New York: Harper and Row Publisher, p.982.
[41] Pessini, A. (1999). Jean-Loup de Virieu Beauvoir ministro plenipotenziario alla corte di Francia durante la rivoluzione. *Aurea Parma*. LXXXIII, pp. 429-451.